Remembering The Porcupine Mountains

By Richard R. Ueck

Michigan Department of Natural Resources District Supervisor, Retired

ISBN-13: 978-1494719494
ISBN-10: 1494719495

Printed in the United States of America.

This journal is dedicated to
Jeanne, my wife of
almost 60 years.
She has smoothed the
bumps from our great
life-long adventure.

Acknowledgements:

Edited by Arthur R. Ueck and Jeanne Ueck.

Forward by Arthur R. Ueck, grandson.

Editing and Formatting by Theresa Sours.

Contents

Forward

Grandpa took a civil service exam during high school for employment with the Department of Conservation. After graduation, he joined the Marine Corps and was sent to Korea. While in Korea, he got notice from the Department that he could report to Lansing for a job interview. Being employed by Uncle Sam, he wrote the Department and asked to be put on the inactive employment list.

When he returned from Korea, he and grandma got married. With the G.I. bill he enrolled in college. During his summers at college he worked for the Department of Conservation as a seasonal Park Ranger. His first summer was at Rochester Utica State Recreation Area near Pontiac, Michigan. The next two summers were at W.J. Hayes State Park south of Jackson in the Irish Hills. There was no affordable housing available at Hayes so they bought an 8'x10' wall tent and camped. Dad was age one and Aunt Pat was age two the first summer in the tent. Grandma and the kids spent those summers in their bathing suits on the beach at Wampler's Lake.

Grandpa was the night Ranger and kept the park orderly during those hours. They said it was two of the best summers they ever had, tent camping, picnicking and friendships with other campers. They never got rained out.

When Grandpa graduated from the University, the Department sent him to Higgins Lake State Park as a full time Ranger. He spent his first deer season working the club country east of Roscommon.

They were then promoted to the Porcupine Mountain State Park (PMSP) in the Upper Peninsula of Michigan and spent the next six years there. Grandpa said it was the best work experience he had and that it was a dream come true. Most of the stories in the journal were written about their experiences in the Porcupine Mountains.

From the PMSP he was sent as the Park Supervisor to McLain State Park west of Hancock on the Portage Lake entry to Lake Superior. From McLain they were promoted to Lakeport State Park on Lake Huron, north of Port Huron.

Lakeport was a real challenge (1966-1971). Vietnam, Woodstock, pot, endless beer, free love, hippies, motorcycles and the Detroit riots all made for long days and nights for the park's staff. Grandpa said the violations and citations flowed like beer. He got to the point where he couldn't go into the campground because the pot smell made him sick.

January 1971, Grandpa got promoted to the District 12 Waterways Supervisor in Plainwell. This was their home area. Grandma made him promise not to move anymore. Everything they owned was portable because of their ten moves in twelve years. The kids were also having trouble with their schooling and loss of friends. Grandma had her own career with the Department of Conservation. She worked as a State Park Clerk, District Secretary and finished her career as a District Accountant. They were at District 12 for 21 years. Grandpa retired with 34 years of service.

They spend their summers in the shadow of the Porcupine Mountains at their cabin on Lac Vieux Desert in Gogebic County. My sister and I have made many trips into the mountains with Grandma and Grandpa.

A.R. Ueck - 2013

**Map of Porcupine Mountains
Wilderness State Park**
Ontonagon, Michigan

Map by Michigan Department of Natural Resources
Parks and Recreations Division

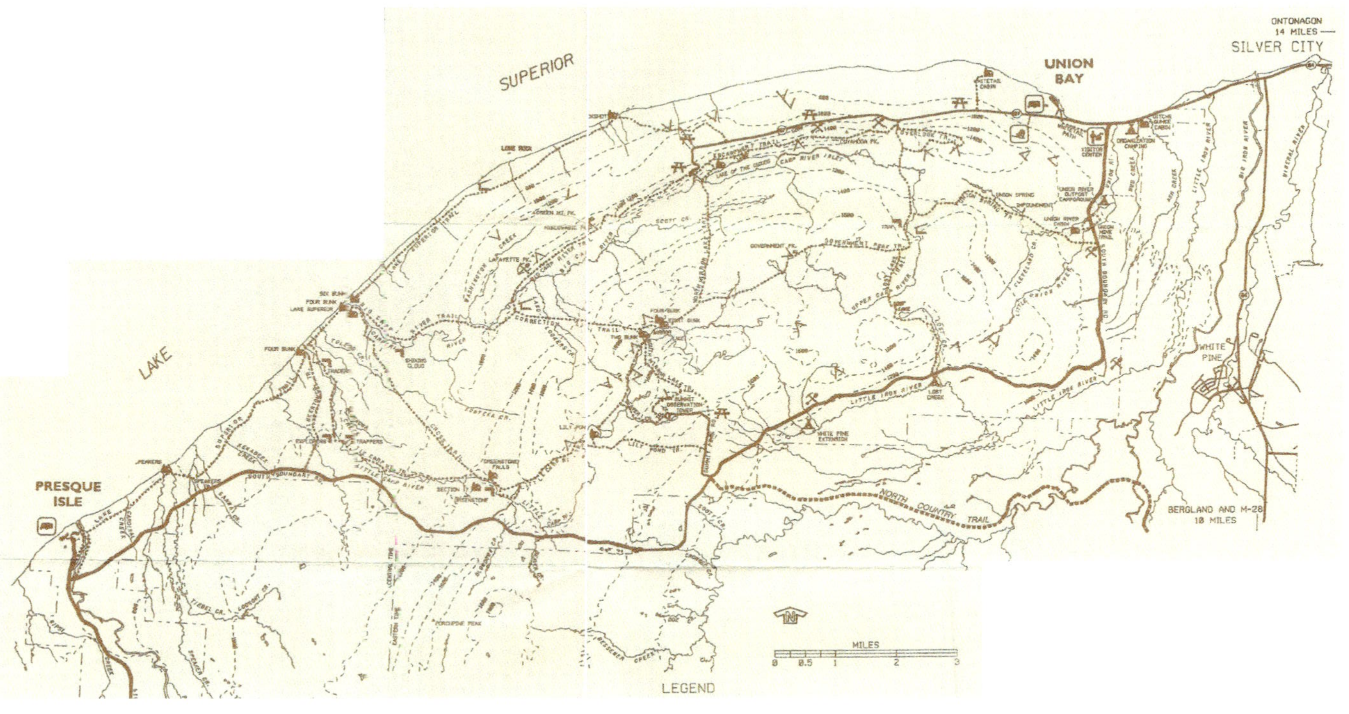
ONTONAGON
14 MILES
SILVER CITY
UNION BAY
SUPERIOR
LAKE
PRESQUE ISLE
WHITE PINE
BERGLAND AND M-28
10 MILES
NORTH COUNTRY TRAIL
LITTLE IRON RIVER
BIG IRON RIVER
SOUTH BOUNDARY RD
VISITOR CENTER
LAKE OF THE CLOUDS
SUMMIT OBSERVATION TOWER
LOST CREEK
WHITE PINE EXTENSION
MILES
0 0.5 1 2 3
LEGEND

Jeanne and Dick Ueck, Lakeport State Park 1969.

Dick, Rich and Pat Ueck with our tent home at W.J. Hayes State Park the summers of 1959 and 1960

CHAPTER 1
A Spot Light

I was working at Higgins Lake State Park during my first deer season with the Department of Conservation. The Regional office in Roscommon assigned me to work law enforcement in Alcona County, out of the department's field office at Lincoln. I partnered up with the local officer, Don Gillies, and worked with him the entire deer season. Don's area included a large portion of the private hunt clubs.

On my first day with him, I was riding shotgun and he told me to reach under my seat and pull out the cigar box. The box was full of club gate keys. From then on, it was my job to open and close club gates. Working clubs was quite an experience. Most of them had large land holdings, some with thousands of acres and some of the club houses looked like hotels and nearly all of their deer blinds were heated.

We were getting deer shining complaints on state land near Lincoln. Don and I drove into the area one evening and parked on a high hill overlooking a good portion of the area where the shining complaints originated. We were there about an hour when we saw a shining light below us and heard a gunshot. We drove down the hill and soon came up behind a well-worn pickup truck. Don hit the red flashing lights of the patrol car and the truck raced on down the old logging road. He hit the siren and they still ran on. We were right on their bumper and I saw a long gun go out the passenger window and hit the ground. Marking the spot as best as I could, we drove on. It was a mile or so later before we got the truck stopped. We got the occupants out of the truck and I watched them by the vehicle lights while Don searched the truck. He could not find a spotlight for evidence to make a shining violation. The occupants were quite interesting, two heavily bearded, beer bottle biologists, dressed for the occasion, and a woman wearing an old cotton, flowered house dress. They were all well fed. The woman was standing between the two men. We questioned them about the shining, gunshot and deer but got no answers. I can still hear Don asking them where the shining light was.

Their answer was, “We don’t have a shining light.”

In those days, spotlights that plugged into the cigarette lighter were very popular and most had a five foot cord. Watching the three subjects, I saw what looked like a spotlight cable hanging down almost to the ground between the woman's legs. The more I looked at it, the more I knew it was the plug end of a spotlight cable. My next move was to bend down in front of her and pretend to re-tie my boot lace. I got down far enough to reach the light cord. I gave it a good hard yank and the nice looking spotlight bounced from between her legs to the ground.

Officer Don said, "That looks like a spotlight to me."

I looked at the faces of her two escorts and thought, boy, are we in for it now. We cooled the situation down and Don issued a shining citation to the driver. The next morning we looked for the dead deer and the tossed gun. We found the beat up old 12 gauge single barrel shotgun, but no deer. No one ever claimed the gun, so it went to State auction. The driver ended up with the only citation.

CHAPTER 2
New Assignment: A Ski Hill

It was early December and the department moved us from Higgins Lake State Park to fill a vacancy at the Porcupine Mountains. It was a quick move because ski season was about to start and the hill needed a new manager. We arrived late on a December afternoon with all our possessions, furniture, cat, dog, two young kids and worn out car.

Knox Jamison, the Park Supervisor, greeted us. He had been the supervisor of the area since it's beginning in 1946 and was also a native of the area. Before Knox became the Park Supervisor he spent a number of years with the Conservation Department's Land Division. It was that expertise the department needed to purchase the sixty thousand acres of the park.

I can still remember saying to him, "I am sorry for all this commotion and confusion", with kids crying, dog and cat squaring off at each other, and Jeanne, my wife, worrying about the new Upper Peninsula experience since she had never been in the U.P. before. Knox said, "don't worry, I've raised three girls and have experienced it all." He then showed us our new quarters. It was the middle apartment of the staff building and had never been lived in. It was beautiful compared to anything we had lived in since college. The picture window looked out over Union Bay on Lake Superior.

After we got settled, I went to the park office to get my new assignments. It turned out to be the greatest job and learning experience I ever had. My position was Assistant Park Supervisor, Porcupine Mountains State Park. The park is the crown jewel of the Michigan park system.

Knox told me what my assignment was. He gave me complete charge of the ski area. I had never before seen or been on a ski hill, so it was a challenge. When he said 'complete charge', *complete* charge he meant. I saw very little of him the next three months during the ski season.

Our ski hill was about a quarter of a mile up M-107 from the park office. When I laid eyes on it, the hill was an awesome sight. There were T-bar lifts and buildings, beautiful chalet constructed by the park staff and inmates, several ski runs and a large open slope with several rope tows. Two large parking lots were below the chalet. The hill had a 300 foot vertical drop, the highest in the midwest. The view coming down the hill was spectacular, as it looked out over Lake Superior. The facility was constructed and financed by the state park system to prove to the local area that skiing could bring big business to the area.

A Austrian made T-bar was the main tow to the top of the mountain. The Europeans were the only manufacturers of ski lifts in those days. We would order our spare parts for the T-bar early in the spring for the next year's season. Parts and maintenance to the lifts were a problem.

Ford industrial gas engines powered all of the ski lifts. Electrical power for the lifts was not available at that time. Running with gas power was difficult and expensive, even in those days.

Potable water for the chalet was also a problem. A small spring and storage tank serviced the hill. The solid rock of the mountain made water well drilling impossible. The chalet had a large stone fireplace, warming areas, food, ski rental and sales concession, plus a ski patrol room that was my office. Large picture windows faced the mountain and it's ski runs, a magnificent sight.

Being the hill manager, I was also the ski patrol leader. We used mainly young, good skiing locals for the patrol. They were trained in first aid. I did, however, get to know just about every skiing doctor in the midwest. We would use them for consultation when we had a bad injury on the hill. Ski patrol and doctors would ski free. Ski injuries were our greatest concern. We would get almost 100 injuries during a season. Knee and ankle sprains were the most common, with broken leg bones next and then ski edge cuts. The kind of injury determined how we gave them first aid. A suspected sprain or broken bone got splinted. Edge cuts got compressed bandages. They were then sent to the hospital in Ontonagon or White Pine. We only had two doctors in the local area. On heavy ski use days, I would call each hospital to find out if they had a doctor on call. If they did, I would send the injured to that hospital. We would load the injured in a private car and transport them. Ambulances were scarce in those days, so we never used them.

Staffing and running the ski area was done by seasonal park rangers from various state parks in the U.P. We had 10 of them and they were the cream of the crop of the seasonal employees. They ran the rope tows, handed out T-bars and sat in the crows nests which were the safety shut-off buildings at the top of the lifts. Numerous other hill and chalet tasks were performed by them. Mechanic, Arnold Anderson, kept the two T-bar lifts running, as well as the engines of the rope tows. Ranger, Arne Tapani, kept the rope tow staffed and did maintenance for the chalet. Ranger, Ed Goninan, was in charge of selling lift tickets and motor vehicle permits.

Our seasonal lift tickets were $15.00 for youths and $20.00 per adult. Daily tickets were also available. Compared to today's prices on ski hills, it was a real deal.

If we got fresh snow first thing in the morning, Fire Officer Bud Kingren and I plowed the parking lots and entrance road. We took turns using the Sno-cat to groom the runs on the hill.

Running the ski area was quite a challenge for me. It ran seven days a week for almost 3 months. We would get the large crowds on the weekends, sometimes as high as 15 Greyhound and school buses from all over the mid-west. It was sure great to see the water start running off the hill in the spring.

Ski season in the Porcupine Mountains State Park (PMSP), now called Porcupine Mountains Wilderness State Park. Park entrance sign and Lake Superior.

Pat and Rich Ueck at the top of the PMSP ski area T-bar lift with Lake Superior in the background.

T-bar building and hand painted PMSP sign.

Top of the T-bar lift looking at 300-foot vertical drop.

T-bar building and lift from the chalet.

PMSP "Crow's nest" lift safety shut-off building.

Brad Anderson and Rich Ueck in front of the chalet, 1962.

PMSP upper parking lot ona weekend.

Tucker Sno-cat used for rescue and hill grooming.

Sno-cat used for rescue, maintenance and hill grooming with the chalet behind it.

CHAPTER 3
TV Tower

During the late 50's and early 60's White Pine residents wanted television reception and so did we, the Park residents. White Pine made a proposal to Knox to construct a TV tower behind and west of the ski hill. White Pine offered to pay for the tower and construct it. But the Park being what it is, a wilderness area, drew opposition from Lansing. They said it would be seen from the Lake of the Clouds overlook several miles west of the proposed tower. Knox and White Pine, after much negotiation, convinced the Lansing Park staff that it wouldn't be seen from the overlook. The tower was then approved by Lansing and completed during the winter of 1961 and '62. I am sure that Knox knew the tower would be seen from the overlook, but we all wanted TV so bad that he gambled that it wouldn't. During the winter months, Highway M-107 was not plowed from the ski hill to the Lake of the Clouds, a distance of about seven miles. In March of '62, Knox got worried about the tower being seen from the overlook. He sent me up M-107 with the Parks sno-cat to see if the tower was visible. The seven mile run up to the overlook was quite a workout for me and the sno-cat. Hard packed snow three to four feet deep slowed the assignment. I made it to the, now, ticket booth area and decided to snowshoe the last half mile up the hill to the parking area and overlook. With the white snow and leafless trees, the TV tower was very clear seven miles away. I thought "O-boy" will Lansing make White Pine remove the tower? We were sure enjoying our new TV service.

It took me an hour or two to get back to the Park office on Union Bay (the now Park Trading Post).

Knox greeted me by saying, "Well?"

I replied, "Knox, I saw it pretty good from the overlook."

His reply was "The hell you say?"

After 50 years, I can still hear his remark and see the look on his face. The fur flew a bit from Lansing, but we kept the tower and it's still there. White Pine must have had a little political pull, I think.

Another TV tower story involving a rather large bear:

The underground electric power cable servicing the tower ran from the ski hill chalet to the tower. The cable was buried with little over-burden soil because of the solid rock of the mountain. One day we lost TV power and reception. When we went up the line to the tower, we found that erosion had uncovered a section of the cable. A large bear, about 400 pounds bit into the exposed cable and blew off the top of his head. The bear had shorted the tower out. Power and the TV problem was solved.

CHAPTER 4
Ham or Bacon Bear

When the April trout season opened, we would dispatch two rangers to the Big and Little Carp rivers for fish and park law enforcement. We would team up with two officers out of the Wakefield Department of Conservation office. The hike into the Carps was approximately seven miles from either direction. The Ranger cabin (now the Lake Superior cabin) was our quarters for about a two week period, depending on the fishing pressure. We would get a lot of rainbow trout snagging and other violations at the area.

The trout season arrived and Ranger Jerry Stilson and I got the assignment to hike into the Carps. We chose to hike the Big Carp River Trail rather than the Lake Superior Trail because of the lake's ice and heavy snow pack. Our starting point was the Lake of the Clouds parking lot. If the pack ice left Superior and we got fair weather, we would be picked up by boat in a week or two. Each of us was carrying about 40 lbs. of food, gear, extra clothes, sleeping bag, etc. in our Duluth pack sacks. As I remember, it was rough going, lots of hard pack snow and a very wet trail. Crossing the Big Carp river about two thirds of the way was a particular challenge. We found a fallen tree across the roaring river and shimmied across it with our packs and everything else we were carrying. About six hours later, we reached the ranger cabin; it was a wonderful sight, located at the mouth of the Big Carp with Lake Superior 200 feet away. The then, Dick Cabin (now Carp Lake 6 -Bunk) was across the river from the Ranger Cabin. A small stringer cedar bridge crossed the river at that location. It was a beautiful remote area, one of my most memorable areas of the park.

Our cabin was small, about 12x14 foot, with a wood cook stove and two wooden bunk beds. Jerry and I got a fire started and arranged our gear. It wasn't long when the two officers arrived from the Wakefield Office. We all were carrying pre-arranged food in our packs to keep us fed for a week or two. Keeping our perishable foods cold at that time of the year wasn't much of a problem. Lake Superior was one big refrigerator. One of the cabin windows had a large shelf on the outside with a wooden box on it to hold our perishables. We would open the window and use what we needed out of the box. It wasn't a very complicated refrigerator. Our canned goods that needed cooling were stashed in the river.

I was in the cabin by myself one late afternoon fixing supper, while the others were on the rivers keeping fisherman orderly. As I fussed with the meal, I could hear noises outside at the window food box. When I looked out, I saw a rather large bear trying to open the box. By the time I armed myself with the cabin straw broom, the bear had the box open and was stealing meat. We had a ham and a couple of pounds of bacon in it. I got the window open, pushed the broom at him, got him running, but not before he grabbed the ham. I saved the bacon, but he got the best of the deal.

A note about The Raymond Dick Cabin:

It was there in the very early 40's that a small number of dedicated sportsman and conservationists had a vision that the Porcupine Mountains should be dedicated as a Federal or State Park. In 1946, the Michigan Legislature appropriated one million dollars to create the Porcupine Mountains State Park.

The Raymond Dick cabin is now the PMSP Big Carp 6-Bunk cabin and bridge across the mouth of Big Carp River.

Put your pack on and hike into the mouth of the Big Carp River. Dick Ueck 50 years ago.

Big Carp River Ranger Cabin and Author 50 years ago.

Big Carp River Ranger Cabin (2009) now called the Lake Superior Cabin.

CHAPTER 5
National Geographic Deer

National Geographic was doing a series of stories about unique state parks in various states, the Porcupine Mountains was chosen for Michigan. When the photographers, Albert Moldvay (National Geographic) and Bob Harrington (Dept. of Conservation) showed up at the park to do the story, Knox gave me the duty to escort them throughout the park. It was late winter, a beautiful time for a photo series. I worked with them for about a week. We used the Sno-cat and snowshoes to get to the remote areas of the park. Lake of the Clouds overlook was a promising location as was Mirror Lake. They took thousands of pictures. We even had two of our Department airplanes up and they photographed from the air.

I had a really good beagle and was hunting almost every evening after work. We had several rabbits aging on my porch.

When the photographers would come over to my apartment for warming or coffee, they would admire the rabbits in a tasteful way, saying how well they liked rabbit stew. My wife, Jeanne is a very good cook, homemade bread and pie maker, and most of all, she makes great rabbit stew. On the last day of the parks photo shoot, I invited the two of them over for rabbit stew. Jeanne put on a great meal for them. They ate like it was the best meal they had in a month.

After the meal, one of them looked out our apartment picture window and said, "Look at those deer."

I said, "Those are our pets that we feed daily", about a dozen of them.

You never saw cameras come out so fast and both photographers began taking pictures. Our young kids, Pat and Rich, were looking out the window at the deer and became the photographer's subjects. Kids, deer, Lake Superior and snow, it was perfect. It must have been a perfect scene because a few months later it appeared on the cover of the November 1963 National Geographic Journal (magazine). It is also the centerfold.

National Geographic Society magazine cover photo by Albert Moldvay, featuring Rich and Pat Ueck.

Photos from the Ueck apartment, courtesy of Michigan Department of Natural Resources by Robert Harrington photographer. Pictured are Dick, Jeanne, Pat and Rich Ueck.

Photos from the top of the escarpment PMSP. Michigan Department of Natural Resources by Robert Harrington.

CHAPTER 6
Pinkerton Trail

Before the South Boundary Road was completed, the Big and Little Carp cabins were some of the most remote areas of the park. We had a small bridge over the Big Carp at its mouth. The Little Carp was really remote and bridgeless, so the only way you could cross it at the cabin and Lake Superior Trail was to wade it or shimmy a log somewhere up stream.

When the South Boundary Road was completed west of Pinkerton Creek, Knox decided to push a foot trail north from the South Boundary to the Little Carp cabin and Superior Trail. This would shorten the hiking distance from about seven miles to two and a half. It would also give us a shorter access for construction of a bridge across the Little Carp River at the cabin and trail.

The trail and cabin ranger, Arne Tapani and I took compass and map, blazed a trail due north from the now Pinkerton Trail head to the Little Carp cabin. It was a straight shot north, but now it meanders a bit for easier walking.

With the trail marked, Knox sent Arne, Arnold Anderson (Park Mechanic), Ed Goninan (Ranger) and me to the Little Carp to construct a bridge across the river at its mouth. We stayed in the cabin for three weeks constructing the bridge.

It was constructed with white cedar, cut and floated down the shoreline to the location at the river mouth. We peeled, split, cut and shaped all the cedar by hand. An inmate crew from Camp Porcupine (prison camp) would come in once a week to help us with the heavy work. The bridge, like the one in the movie "The Bridge on the River Kawai" was a beautiful thing. All native cedar, two rock cribs constructed in the river filled with river and shore rocks, stringers and hand split walk treads with hand rails.

Three years after its construction, Lake Superior ice jams took it out. The only thing left of it is the pictures I took when it was completed. A new suspension bridge now replaces it, a short distance from the original location.

Rock and cedar crib was the beginning of the first bridge across the Little Carp River, 1962.

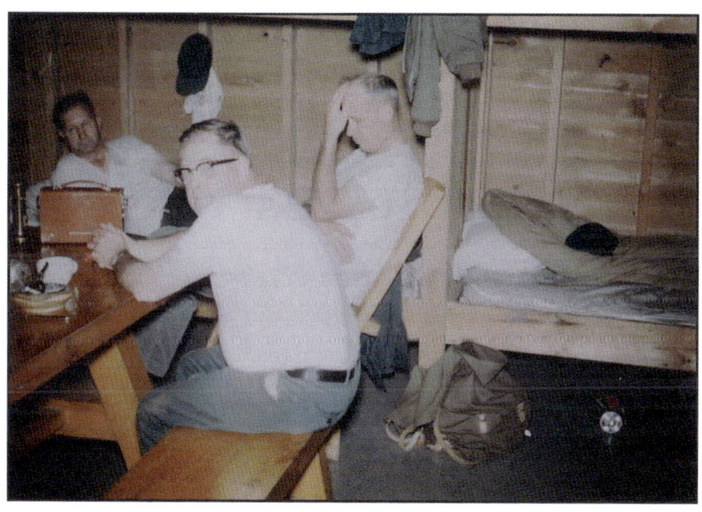

Inside the Little Carp River cabin. Left to right: Rangers Arne Tapani, Ed Goninan and Arnold Anderson.

Completed Little Carp River bridge, 1962.

Log jam above the bridge, 1963.

Little Carp River cabin with Author, granddaughter Hil and grandson A.R., fifty years later.

The new Little Carp River suspension bridge (2010) up stream from the first bridge.

CHAPTER 7
A Lynx

During deer season, I usually worked the area east of Lake Gogebic with Officer Ken Grant. One of our most heavily used areas was the Matchwood Tower Road (now U.S. Forest Service Road 6930). The East Shore Road of Lake Gogebic was not yet constructed. The Tower Road was the nearest serviceable access road to the area east of Lake Gogebic. The trees, mostly hemlock served as a large winter deer yard and great hunting area with slash areas (cut over timber) surrounding it. The Tower Road had a small campground at the Matchwood Fire Tower with about a dozen sites which grew to at least 20 during deer season. The campground had a well and hand pump, the only palatable water in the area. If we stayed there long enough, we would see 95 percent of the hunters in the area getting their drinking water.

Portable deer camps along the Tower Road were numerous, 50 or so from the fire tower to Sleepy Hollow to the East. There were also a number of permanent camps inland from the road. They were old converted logging camps, cabins and a trapper shack or two.

We would check most of these camps before and during the deer season. It was a great duty, because we got to talk to the hunters and check out their many unique camps. Checking camps always involved looking at the dead deer hanging on the meat poles (a pole or trees where the hunters hung their deer). Our main concern was unsealed or improperly sealed deer.

In those days, there was a bounty paid by the state for coyote, fox and bobcats (lynx were protected as they are today). During one of these camp meat pole checks, I came across, what I thought was a Canadian Lynx hanging on the meat pole.

I questioned the proud hunter and said, “Would you take five dollars for that bobcat?” Five dollars was the state bounty for a bobcat.

The hunter answered a proud “Yes.”

I knew then, that he really thought he had shot a bobcat. A lynx is a pretty big cat with long legs, large claws, tuffs on his ears and a black tip on his tail. Their fur is lighter in color than a bobcat. I had seen a number of bobcats, but never a lynx. I told the hunter that I didn’t think he had a bobcat and that I thought it was a lynx, but to be sure I would have it checked. We had a department biologist working out of the Wakefield office and he confirmed it was a lynx. The cat was confiscated by the state and no citation was issued to the hunter. It was a beautiful specimen and very rare in our state.

CHAPTER 8
Toilet Building Bear

We lived in the center apartment of the park's staff quarters on Union Bay. The area was frequented by black bears during the camping season. Every campsite in the Union Bay Campground had a trash basket and the bears got really smart toward trash basket lunches. To control nuisance bears, we had a live bear trap behind the staff quarters. It was a culvert trap about 36" in circumference and six feet long with a sliding metal trap door on one end and a welded steel grate on the other. The trigger for the trap was inside and the bait hung on the trigger cable. The bears liked sardines, the expensive cross packed oil kind, so that is what I used for bait. I could catch any bear in Carp Lake Township with a good can of the little fish. The trap was always set in camping season and I would start catching bears, skunk and other critters during the season, but usually the largest bears first. The smaller bears were caught at the end of the season. When we caught a bear, we would transport it and let it loose as far away from the campground as possible. We let some go close to Lake Gobebic State Park to create some excitement for their staff and campers. I don't think the Gogebic staff ever put two and two together. I never told them! I always wondered if they, too, were sending critters our way.

We were getting complaints from the Union Bay campers that a very large bear was creating excitement for the camps in the evening shortly after dark. So, I took the truck into the campground on an evening with complaints and sure enough I spotted the bear on the campground road next to the toilet building. He was large, about 450 lbs. by my estimate, and one of the biggest I ever dealt with. I got up to him and honked the trucks horn but nothing happened! I think he would have confronted the truck. My next move was to put the truck's front bumper just as close to him as possible and give him a good bump and push. That got him out of the campground and into the woods, but I could still hear him moaning and chomping his teeth. But it did get rid of him for that night.

A complaint came in the next night that the same bear had the women pinned in the toilet building and wouldn't let them out.

"What now?" I thought.

Maybe I could walk him to the bear trap behind the

staff quarters. I grabbed my 12 gauge Winchester shotgun loaded with 00 buckshot and a can of good sardines, then off to the campground I walked. When I got to the toilet building, sure enough, there he was blocking ingress and egress to the women's toilet. I got as close to him as possible. With the Winchester pointing his direction, I opened the sardine can enough to start dripping sardine oil toward the bear trap which was about 200 yards away. I moved toward it very slowly, dripping oil and keeping an eye on the villain. He moved with me smelling the oil at the distance of about 25 yards. The trap was previously set so, when I reached it, I slid the sardine can in the trap and went into my apartment to watch out my rear window. It didn't take 10 minutes and I had the toilet building bear in the trap. With his fear and brute strength, he started breaking the welds on the trap's door and rear gate, but they held.

In the morning, the inmate crew reluctantly loaded the trap, with the bear still inside, onto the truck for transport. We wanted to move him as far as possible to the interior of the park to prevent him from returning. Park Fire Officer, Bud Kingren, had a large Walker Beagle named "Boozer" and I had my beagle "Nick". We often used them to run bears from the area. Bud and I, with our dogs, trucked the bear as far as possible to the interior of the park. We released the bear and put both dogs on his heels. They ran out of the area and we spent several hours getting our dogs back. As far as I know, the bear never returned.

Culvert wheeled bear trap with grandkids, Arthur and Hil Ueck.

We had bear jams, not traffic jams in 1963.

I wouldn't recommend this feeding procedure. PMSP 1962.

CHAPTER 9
Witness Tree

Lost Lake Trail ran from the Lost Creek outpost campground north to Lost Lake where it ended. We decided that we could extend it to the Government Peak trail giving access to more of the parks trail system. Knox wanted to connect it so we picked a good leafless spring day to do the ground work. He ran compass and I did the trail marking. We used the square orange, metal trail marking tags. The tags had two nail holes in them so you could nail them to a tree. We would place them about eye level within sight of each other.

That area of the park was part of William A. Burt's original Upper Peninsula survey in 1847 and Knox had copies of Burt's survey. Our trail ran almost due north towards Government Peak. As I remember it from over 50 years ago, we were in the general location of where sections 25, 30, 31 & 36 converged. Somewhere in that general area we came across an original witness tree with Burt's 1847 markings. Knox chopped the 100 plus years of bark away from the blaze and Burt's writing was clearly visible. I think the tree was a large sugar maple. After the witness tree, we continued marking until we reached the Government Peak trail to connect the two trails.

Another note about Government Peak:

We had a complaint that there was no sign on the peak. Someone took it or else a bear mangled it, which often happened. So, trail Ranger Arne Tapani and I got the assignment to replace the sign. As I remember, it was about 90 degrees, humid and the biting stable flies were mad and about the size of humming birds. We hiked in from the Union Spring trail with a new routed "Government Peak" sign. When we got to Trap Falls, Arne suggested that we cut a cedar post for the new sign because he knew there wasn't any cedar on Government Peak. We cut and peeled a post. Arne carried the routed wood sign, axe, and shovel, which were the tools necessary to set a new sign. I carried the fresh cut, wet post up the two and a half miles to the 1,850 foot summit of Government Peak. When we reached the summit, there stood the most perfect, politically correct, signless post in the park. Seeing the empty post, we fixed the sign. At least I got my morning exercise. I stashed the new post for future use.

After all of my effort, some hiker/camper probably got some easy-to-gather firewood.

Arne and I were both suffering. He said to me, "Would you like a beer?"

I answered a growling "Yea", thinking of Macs and Stubbs bars in Ontonagon or Pauls Bar in Silver City.

Arne reached into his pack sack and brought out two Gobels Bantam beers, about 6 ounces each. I couldn't believe it. That beer saved my life. Arne knew we had a hot, rough assignment and he was well prepared.

CHAPTER 10
Governor's Guide

During the early 60's, dark clouds were forming over the park. The local "Anti's" and their legislators wanted to extend highway M-107 along Lake Superior across the Carp's and Presque Isle rivers towards the Black River area. It would have cut the heart out of the mountains. They also wanted to open it to copper mining again. The parks virgin timber was also on the chopping block. Governor George Romney was being pressured by the Lower Peninsula to save and preserve the wilderness area. He was getting a lot of opposition from both ends, so he decided to take a look for himself at the park and area. When the Governor and his entourage arrived in the park, Regional Park Supervisor Glenn Gregg ordered me to volunteer to escort the Governor and crew across the mountains. Glenn introduced me to "Mac".

I said, "Mac who?"

Glenn sheepishly said, "Ralph McMullen, the Director of our Conservation Department."

I could tell I made a big impression with my two bosses, but I was a youngster in the Department. I lived 600 miles from Lansing and never met a Director before.

When the Governor arrived at the Lake of the Clouds parking lot, the staging area of the hike, Director McMullen introduced me to Governor Romney. The Governor said little to me as newspaper and television cameras were buzzing. He had numerous interviews.

I was told by Glenn to take the North Mirror Lake trail to Mirror Lake, then go South on the South Mirror Lake trail to the Summit Peak road. It was the distance of about six miles. The weather was warm, about 80 degrees. I was carrying a canteen and so was the Governor. He looked in good shape in his 50's and he had the reputation of being a jogger. I was also in good shape, having hiked almost daily while working in the park.

When the hike finally got started, it looked like a safari with all its porters, TV camera men, newspaper reporters, politicians, body guards, Department officials, etc. Down the escarpment we went crossing, the Big Carp foot bridge and the Governor set a fast pace.

After about 15 minutes, the Governor said to me, "Let's go. I want to get rid of those people."

We set a real fast pace, almost a run. We got way ahead of the rest of the party and couldn't hear them anymore. He started talking to me and asking numerous questions about the park and local politics. I had about three and a half hours with him, no politicians, no news people or others. We took a breather at Mirror Lake and he seemed very impressed with the beauty of the area. He really was a good listener and very knowledgeable about the park. When we got to the end of the hike about four hours later, he had worked up a sweat and seemed quite tired. He thanked me and was on his way to the next political problem. When Director McMullen and Glenn Gregg left the park, I asked them if we had won the battle.

Glenn answered, “I think we did.”

Indeed we did win - no mining, no tree cutting and no road extension to this date.

A few weeks later, I got a very nice note from Director McMullen and the Governor. Several months later, I got a promotion from the Regional Park Director Glenn Gregg.

Senator Joe Mack (Ironwood), Governor George Romney and the governor's guide, Officer Dick Ueck.

CHAPTER 11
Cabin Key

During our time at the Porkies, we had eight interior wilderness cabins. You had to hike to all of them and some were accessible by boat in good weather. They were from three fourths of a mile hike (Lake of the Clouds cabin) and as far as 7 miles (Carp cabins). Mirror Lake was about two and a half miles from the Summit Peak Road.

Rental reservations were taken in advance for the cabins. When the ranger checked a cabin out to a visitor, he had a list of instructions and information for each cabin. He also gave them the proper key for the cabin they requested. The key was very important because of obvious reasons.

John was a young, first season ranger working in the office assigning visitors to their cabins. His father was the departments Regional Business Executive for the whole U.P. In other words, he was big brass. This was John's first time away from home and his mother and dad would visit him a couple of times a month to see how he was doing. His dad would always get me aside and ask how his son was getting along and requested that I would take care of him. I would always give him a positive, reassuring answer.

On one particular weekend, John checked out the Mirror Lake 4-Bunk Cabin to the renter and forgot to give them the cabin key. About an hour later John remembered that he forgot the key. He came to me and told me about it and he asked me what he should do. My answer to him was to get the truck and drive to the Mirror Lake parking lot and hike the two and a half miles to the cabin and give the renters the key. Hopefully, he would catch the users before they got to the cabin or when they were coming back out for the forgotten key. John had to hike the two and a half miles to the cabin and got there just as the renters discovered that they didn't have the key. John made their day with the personal delivery.

During his dad's next visit to the park, he got me aside and told me that he was no longer worried about his son. The hike with the key to Mirror Lake was one of the best lessons he ever had. He also told me that he knew I was taking care of him.

CHAPTER 12
A Close Gunshot

Officer Ken Grant and I were working deer hunters west of Lake Gogebic. We were in the process of checking a travel trailer camp when I came across an improperly sealed doe on their meat pole. I brought it to Ken's attention and he said to check out the trailer and see if any of the hunters were home. Standard operation procedure was for one officer to cover the back of the camp and the other would knock on the door. Ken took the back and I proceeded to knock on the door. About the second knock, a loud gunshot rang out and being a former Marine that was in the Korean War, I was immediately flat on the ground. When I got the nerve to move, I started patting myself all over to find out where I was hit.

Seconds later Ken was at my side and said, "Dick, are you okay?"

I answered, "I think so." I defensively got up.

He yelled loud to the occupant of the camper, "State Officers! Open the door!"

The door opened and a sheepish hunter appeared.

Ken asked, "Who is doing the shooting?"

The hunter replied, "Me. I was unloading my rifle when I saw you officers checking the deer and I didn't want a citation for a loaded gun in the camper."

He said that he knew the deer was improperly sealed and thought he was going to get a ticket for it. He was right, he got a citation for the unsealed deer. After questioning him, we thought we figured out what happened. When he saw me coming to the door, he was frantically trying to unload his Winchester lever action 30-30. The only way you can unload a rifle of that style is to work the lever action until the rifle is empty. If you happen to pull the trigger during the unloading process the rifle could fire. In his nervous excitement, he pulled the trigger during the unloading process and he fired the rifle. The careless shot went through the trailer door, about six inches from where I was standing as I knocked on the door. It was heart high.

That afternoon, Ken and I visited the Justice of the Peace that took care of fines in our area. We told him of our experience with the hunter. When the hunter came to pay his fine, the Justice gave him the maximum fine for the incident. We confiscated the deer and gave it to a needy family.

CHAPTER 13
Seven Does

It was the first antlerless deer season in our area and we were working the Matchwood Tower Road. The doe killing brought out the worst of sportsmanship with the hunters. At least, that was my assessment of the season. In some areas, "hunters" would shoot does until a buck was killed and then seal the buck. If a doe was killed and the hunter saw one of us officers coming he would seal the doe. If no officer, the doe laid, unsealed and wasted. In those days the department issued a metal tag with the deer license. The tag was numbered to correspond with the hunters license. It was about 10" long with a locking device on one end and a locking latch on the other, so when you pushed them together they locked tightly. Some violators hung does on the meat pole with the metal tag in the ear or jaw, then pushed the tag together so it looked locked. If they shot a buck they would take a doe off the pole, dispose of it, retrieve the tag and properly lock the tag on the buck. The violators never figured an officer would check the poles for improperly sealed deer, but we did.

Ken and I were checking a large camp and meat pole that had a number of deer hanging. I, being the younger officer, was climbing and checking the seals on each deer. The first seal I pulled popped open.

I said "Kenny, I got one". The second seal pulled also popped open.

"Kenny I got another." He chuckled and said "good!"

This happened five more times that day. We ended up with seven improperly sealed does. Some citations were written, and some does were confiscated. Those confiscated were given to needy families.

CHAPTER 14
South Boundary Road

During my stay in the park, the last 22 miles of the South Boundary Road was completed from Nonesuch to the Presque Isle River. This included the Presque Isle River vehicle bridge. Black topping was done at a later date.

Knox and I did the road right of way survey work from Nonesuch to White Pine Extension. This included the virgin white pine stand between the two. Knox ran compass and I marked the trees that were to be cut. We also estimated the value of the trees. When we got to the white pine stand, the Lansing Parks Division staff got involved. They were not going to let any of the wonderful old pines be cut unless absolutely necessary. I don't know how many times they modified the road location trying to save the pines. I think everyone from the Lansing Engineering Staff and division brass came up to look over the road location. After much looking and head scratching, they settled on the location. I think we only cut one pine and the park carpenter, Al Hanson, confiscated the tree for window and door casings, paneling and park furniture. He guarded the pine lumber like it was gold.

After the survey was completed, two contracts were issued for clearing the right of way. One contract was given to cut and harvest the timber. The second was for clearing, stump removal and grading the area. As with most good government contracts, the local Democratic contractor got the stumping contract and the local Republican contractor got the timber contract. Lansing should have issued me a black and white referee shirt, because that's what I felt like over the next few months while keeping them apart and getting the job done.

Fire Officer Joe Anthony and one of the giant white pines.

Clearing and cutting the trees on the South Boundary Road, 1964.

CHAPTER 15
Airplane Crash

These next two incidents were given to me as second-hand information.

During the middle 40's, a United States Air Force military B-17 bomber crashed in the interior of the park. It's several airman all parachuted to safety and found their way to Silver City. Soon after the crash, parts, aluminum and other items were scavenged by local citizens. This went on until the park got it stopped, but not before almost all of it was removed.

When I visited the site over fifty years ago there were only a few small scattered parts of the plane that hadn't been taken. I could still see the hair cut the timber got when it crashed.

Anyone who has checked out one of the old park cabins has found that the key to the cabin has a thick aluminum tag, about 5"x3" in size, with the cabin's name stamped on it. That aluminum came from the bomber. There is a propeller from the bomber that can be seen at a gift shop in Silver City.

Another plane crash happened on the frozen, snow-covered Lake of the Clouds. A young pilot flying a small ski-equipped Piper Cub landed on the lake. I was informed that when a ski equipped plane lands on snow, the heat friction of the skis will freeze them to the snow or ice. That is apparently what happened. When he tried to take off, the plane was frozen to the ice. His method of getting it unfrozen was to prop the engine throttle open at a reasonable speed, get out of the plane and shake the wings to break the skis free. When it broke free he couldn't get back in the airplane and it taxied and tried to take-off without him. It finally ended up in the brush and trees at the end of the lake. He had a pair of cross country skis tied on the plane so he used them to ski the seven miles to the park office. Several days later, with help, he fixed and flew the plane out.

CHAPTER 16
Stuck

It was a dark overcast day and Officer Grant and I were way back on an old logging road when it started to snow hard. The flakes were about the size of maple leaves. The old road was rough and remote. We started out and a little way down the road we met a hunter who also was heading out. Ken asked him if he wanted a ride, so he jumped in the car. It wasn't long before we met a couple more hunters and they got in. The more it snowed, the more hunters Ken piled into the car. We even had them riding on the front fenders.

I finally mumbled to Ken and asked what he was doing. We had a full vehicle and couldn't haul any more.

He replied to me, "just wait and see." It wasn't long before we got really stuck in a snow filled mud hole. Ken said to the hunters, "everybody out and give a push."

Push they did and we got free of the hole. I then thought to myself, 'now I know why Kenny provided the bus service.' After we reached the main road the hunters got out and thanked us, Ken chuckled and said, “at least we weren’t stuck long.”

CHAPTER 17
A Legislator

Officer Grant and I were working deer hunters on the old logging roads in the Sisson Lilley Creek area. It was a quiet, nice hunting day. We found a good fork in the road where we could check hunter vehicles coming in and going out. We hid our vehicle and worked on foot. Ken took one fork of the road and I took the other, putting us about 50 yards apart. Our strategy was to conceal ourselves and listen for vehicles coming in or out. The roads were in poor shape, so the vehicles had to move slowly. When a vehicle came by one of us, we would move out from behind our concealment, then look into the passenger side of the vehicle for uncased guns and any other violations.

I wasn't at my location long when I heard a vehicle slowly chugging up the road toward me. When it got near me I jumped out and was surprised at what I saw. It was an old Jeepster with two hunters in it. The one in the shotgun seat I recognized immediately. He was a well known state legislator and he also recognized me.

He said to me, "Dick, how come you are moving so fast?"

I answered something like, "I always move fast."

He then said, "do you want a cup of coffee?"

I replied, "no, just had one."

"How about some snoose?" was his next question.

"No, I don't use snoose," was my answer.

During the conversation period, he was stuffing his rifle in it's case. He didn't try to unload it because he knew I was watching.

Ken heard the vehicle and conversation from his location and came over to see what was happening. He was also well acquainted with the legislator. I got Ken aside and told him that I had seen the legislator with an uncased, loaded rifle and asked him, "now what?" I knew we had a hot potato on our hands. Ken, being a long-term senior officer, and I, being a young upcoming one, he advised me that I had a long distinguished career ahead of me in the department and that I was the judge and jury with what I saw and what to do.

I knew what he was telling me and when I approached the legislator, I said, "have a good day hunting." With that, they drove on up the trail.

Later, Ken said, "young man, you made the right decision and you will never regret it."

CHAPTER 18
Folk School

In the early 60's, the Folk School building was constructed for the purpose of a sign and carpenter shop. The Porcupine Mountains State Park (PMSP) as it was called in those days, constructed the wooden park signs for all the State parks in the Upper Peninsula. The 40 man inmate crew housed at Camp Porcupine, just east of Silver City was the labor for the signs. The oldest signs that I remember were carved by hand with raised letters. Carved signs became too time and labor consuming, thus the power routed signs used today replaced them. Signs were constructed during the cold weather months. Building space for making them became a problem and that prompted the construction of the carpenter shop.

Carpenter Foreman Al Hanson was in charge of signs and building construction like the Chalet, Mirror Lake cabins and all the older buildings of the park. Cold weather was sign building time. Al usually had a five or six man crew of the more talented inmates that did the routing.

In order to build the shop, Al had to gather the materials. Pine and hemlock was the principal lumber. The logs to make the lumber were gathered from various locations in the park and sent to Camp Baraga to be sawn and prepared. Camp Baraga was our Parks Division saw mill located near Baraga. Most of the Parks Division lumber used for building construction in those days was milled there. The mill used inmates from Camp Baraga.

During the early 60's when enough lumber and etc. was gathered, construction work began on the building. There was no master plan for the building. Al built it to his needs and specifications. It was several months after its completion that Lansing Park Division discovered it. Some fur flew between Lansing and the Park staff, but the building stayed and was a great asset to the Park.

Another winter project in those days was the making of cedar shingles (shakes) in the park. All of the cedar shingles for state park buildings were cut in the Porkies shingle mill. Two sizes were cut, 14" and 16". The shingle mill was located off the South Boundary Road near the parking lot of the Union Spring Trail. Cedar to make the shingles was cut in various locations. Some were cut just north of the ski hill in the Commission Boundary of the Park. A considerable amount of stock was cut on state land up at Point Abbaye. Inmates from Camp Porcupine ran the shingle mill. Foreman Jerry Beck was their supervisor. Sometime in the middle 60's the mill was moved to Camp Baraga because of the availability of cedar in the Point Abbaye area.

Camp Porcupine was closed down in the middle 60's due to the lack of potable water.

New routered entrance sign.

Old hand-carved, raised letter entrance sign of 50 years ago.

CHAPTER 19
Log Marks

In the spring after the Ontonagon River returned to its normal flow, Jeanne, the kids, and I would canoe the river looking for log marks. Log marks were to loggers what cattle brands were to cattlemen.

During the white pine logging era from 1890 to approximately 1910, the logging companies would have spring log drives on the river. There was a number of companies making those drives. In order to know their particular logs, a company would stamp the end with a log mark (brand). They would use an axe like tool with their particular brand on it's hammer head to mark the logs. The larger logs were usually stamped 5 times on each end, once on the center and again on each quarter, so that when it was floating, one of the brands would be up and visible at all times. They were sorted at the end of the drive. Some rustling took place. Diamond Match, the biggest company, had the most registered marks on the Ontonagon. Their marks were usually diamond-shaped with numbers or letters in the diamond to designate which of their logging camps had cut the log.

These log marks were registered in the Ontonagon County Court House. I think you can still register a mark for 25 cents.

Canoeing the river, we would always take a bow saw with us. When we came across an old pine log with a mark on it, we would cut the mark end off. About 50 of these marks decorate our cabin walls.

Log mark from the Ontonagon River, possibly one from the Holt Lumber Company - OHO.

Author cutting a log mark on the Ontonagon River. This mark is the same one as above. Also pictured are Rich and Pat with our canoe "Red", 1964.

CHAPTER 20
A Bear Once Beagled

Some people think beagles are nice little doggies that smile a lot and wag their tails in circles. That is not always so.

While working as Assistant Manager at Porcupine Mountains State Park some years ago, my wife and I lived in one of the residence buildings in the park. Before we were married, Jeanne was more or less tuned to city life, so residence in the most remote, wildest state parks in Michigan was a new and, as it turned out, thrilling experience for her.

There were many wild animals in our lives during the time we were there, and every darned one of them has a story to tell about his encounter with Mrs. Ueck, who also has a few stories of her own. Most of these animals were the small or middle-sized variety and not much match for brooms, pans, and hurled household objects. But one was a particularly large, ferocious bear, with bristly black fur, long teeth, and a wild look in his eye. This bear probably weighed about a thousand pounds, or more. He would turn up when I was not at home. Jeanne never elected to try small-animal control measures against him, and mostly he just rambled on and off our back yard, front yard, and porch for about half of one summer. Until Bin, that is.

Bin was a so-called lady beagle of good breeding, who stood nine inches high. She probably weighed 12 pounds soaking wet, 9-1/2 dry. Her blood lines were good, she had what might be termed a lovely rabbit-trail howl, and she was an easy keeper. She was also fun to be with and consequently became as much a house pet as she was my rabbit chaser. She liked to ride in cars and trucks so travelled with us a lot. During rabbit season, I could stand in one spot and listen to that string of distant hoots as she circled a rabbit from one side of a swamp to another. You could tell how excited she was by the intensity of those siren wails, and if she got up more than one bunny at a time, it nearly drove her frantic. On cold winter mornings, the rabbits must have enjoyed the romp as much as she did. She never caught any, I seldom shot many, and at the end of the day we would all go home tired and happy.

But for one reason or another, Bin had never met our backyard bear - that thousand-pounder with the lean, hungry, long-toothed look. In fact, we had been somewhat careful about this, because she was obviously no match for such an animal and we didn't want to lose her. So she rode or walked with me when I made trips to remote areas of the park, and she went to town with my wife and fortunately, as it turns out, she did meet it.

Of course we should have known that such a meeting was inevitable, and any plans we had to save little Bin from that awful moment would sooner or later fall apart.

The dreaded moment came one day in late summer, a day that started with a steady downpour. When I left for work that morning, Bin was still asleep in her doghouse in the backyard. Rainy days in state parks are often days for catching up on office work, so Bin couldn't ride with me that day in any case. About 10 A.M., I received a frantic phone call from my wife.

"Quick," she said, "that bear's here again, and Bin's out in the doghouse. I don't know what to do if they get together. Hurry!"

I ran out, jumped in my car and started the two-mile drive home. It was a bumpy, twisting road, and no amount of wishing would make it a fast trip. As I bumped along, all sorts of thoughts passed through my mind. My wife was probably safe enough, as the porch was protected by a stout door. But what if she tried to go out into the yard to save Bin? Or what if the bear got ahold of Bin and she tried to intervene? I shuddered at the thought. I recalled seeing a forlorn and frightened family of campers who had gotten entangled with a bear a few years ago. The bear had apparently become enraged when the campers tried to remove their ice chest from his path. He had smashed the ice chest with one swipe, slashed their tent and knocked it down, and then just out of spite, had thumped an enormous dent into the hood of their Volkswagen, which was near the picnic table.

Another time, two back packers told me they had hung their food packs out of reach on a limb in a small tree as the safest place they could find. That night they were awakened by loud noises, and shining the flashlight from the tent, they saw a huge bear standing beneath the packs, swinging his paws at them. The campers banged pans together and yelled. The bear stood his ground and for a long moment it was a standoff. Finally the bear shuffled away into the woods. Next morning, the campers came out to find that the bottoms of both their packs had been shredded by the bear's sharp and powerful claws, as if someone had slashed the canvas with razor blades. I thought of other stories too, of bear hounds that got too close to their quarry and were ripped to pieces by the powerful animals. Poor little nine-inch high Bin. She wouldn't make much more than a mouthful for a large bear.

As I turned into the driveway and parked, my worst

fears were realized. I heard Bin howling the strangest howl I had ever heard. She was out of sight in the backyard. Racing into the house, I grabbed my deer rifle from the hall closet, picked up some shells, and was headed toward the back door where my wife stood, watching through a window.

"I guess you won't need that," she said with a grin. "As a matter of fact, you have just gained a bear hound and lost a rabbit chaser."

Out the back door window, I saw a pretty silly sight. The bear and the beagle were out there all right, but my fears for Bin's life vanished at a glance. It was the bear that needed the help. Little nine-inch Bin had run that bear up a spindly, willowy, little popple tree. The bear weighed maybe 200 pounds, not even close to 1,000, but it was enough so the tree was bending back and forth under the weight. Bin raced up and down beneath that big black bulge, howling and jumping and trying to nip him in the seat. The bear, meanwhile, kept trying to hitch himself up higher, but he couldn't get much hold on the little tree, and it didn't have many limbs to help him.

When I felt the bear had enough taste of civilization, I went out, caught Bin, and carried her inside. It was like trying to carry an armload of compressed springs, but finally I got her in the house and, after a few minutes, the bear eased himself out of the tree and hurried off into the woods.

After that, we didn't bother to keep Bin separated from the local Bad Bruin. As a matter of fact, he just didn't give us any more trouble, and we didn't see him again for two months. I guess a bear once beagled is twice cautious.

Author's Note:
This story "A Bear Once Beagled" was written in the spring of 1970 and was first published in the November-December 1970 issue of the Michigan Natural Resources magazine. It became so popular that it was published again in the Best of the Michigan Natural Resouces magazine later.

CHAPTER 21
Final Notes

It's been over 50 years since I reported for work at the 60,000 acre Porcupine Mountains State Park. In the days that followed, I hiked all of the 90 miles of the park's foot trails, many of them numerous times. My wife, kids and grandkids have also travelled miles in the interior. On our days off we might rent a vacant cabin and hike or fish for brook trout. All of the cabins were an adventure. Special memories are for Lilly Pond and the Carp River cabins.

Warm, quiet days were spent on the beach hunting agates. We didn't find many, but what we found were nice and went into our fish aquarium. Swimming was rare in Lake Superior, but on hot days we would try. Time was spent at the old copper mines, looking for datolite and native copper. An ancient miner's rock hammer was always a special find.

If Lake Superior was calm and the weather good, we would take our canoe, "Red", west along the shoreline, sometimes as far as Lone Rock. This was especially nice in the fall. The rocky shore, clear water, coloring leaves and solitude was breathtaking.

Early September brought the Steelhead near shore. We would stand out on the rocks near the campground and cast for them. Five to seven pounders were the usual catch and great for eating.

October meant grouse hunting. 'Pats' is the UPer term for them. That was my passion, hunting the park's interior with my dog. GOD made ruffed grouse for the stew pan.

We usually worked law enforcement during deer season, but I always got a day or two off to try for my own buck and often got one.

Ski season brought the area to life. My two children learned to down hill ski and were both great skiers. My son would have been Olympic material, if we had been there longer.

After the day's work at the ski hill, I would take Nick, my beagle, snowshoes and my Winchester to hunt snowshoe hares (rabbits). Not only would we get our share of rabbits, but Nick would run coyotes, bobcats, and whatever she could smell. A few were shot in front of her.

During ski season we had ten or so seasonal rangers living in the park's Seasonal Ranger Quarters and the apartment next to us. Almost every night some of them would be at our quarters for Jeanne's home-made pie or bread and conversation. When we had enough rabbits, Jeanne would make stew and invite them all over. The stew got really popular. If I wasn't hunting, they would ask if they could borrow Nick to see if they could freshen the supply of rabbits for another stew.

Two of our old seasonal rangers were George Stevens and Ernest Keskimaki. They were nightly visitors and provided us with volumes of park, Conservation Department and U.P. history. Their nightly conversations were priceless. They both retired on my watch.

If there was a lot of trail work or heavy maintenance, such as replacing an old wood cooking stove at one of the cabins, I would check out four or five inmates from Camp Porcupine. The camp would provide them with a sack lunch of ham, roast beef, home-made bread, cheese, peanut butter and jelly and black coffee. Jeanne would also pack my lunch on those interior work days, but with the confusion of getting the kids off to school, sometimes things didn't always go right. One particular day the inmates and I sat down for our lunch, they with their ham, beef and home-made bread and me with my lunch bag. I opened my bag and started to eat my sandwich. I thought "that's funny, it tastes like a mustard sandwich", and that's what it was. Jeanne forgot the bologna. I never said a word to the inmates and ate my mustard sandwich while watching them eat their ham, beef and home-made bread. My salivary glands were working overtime and my hunger pains were at a high level, but I said nothing. Another time the coffee ended up being only hot water. When you are six or seven miles into the interior, mustard sandwiches and hot water taste pretty good.

During the last 50 years we have made many trips to the Lake of the Clouds overlook. Each time I see the magnificent view, I get goose bumps. We are extremely thankful that a number of great people saw to it that it was preserved. I consider it a great honor that Jeanne and I have been part of it's history.

Our beagle Nick "Bin" and a couple of snowshoe hares (rabbits), 1962.

The kind of fish that Pat and Rich would catch in Lake Superior, 1962.

Jeanne, Rich and Pat at Lilly Pond 50 years ago.

Grandpa with Rich's children, A.R. and Hil at Lilly Pond almost 50 years later. Note the bear scratches on the siding above and on the side of the sign.

After all the years, I still get goose bumps when I see this view at Lake of the Clouds.

Ueck grandkids at Buckshot Cabin.

Jeanne and the grand-kids on the Big Carp River bridge, outlet of the Lake of the Clouds.

Jeanne and the grandkids with view from the tower at Summit Peak with Lake Superior in the background. At 1,958 feet above sea level it's the highest peak in the park.

Ueck grandkids on the Escarpment Trail west.

Porcupine Mountains fluters, Chris Anderson, Jeanne, Knox and Kate Jamison, 1963.

Jeanne, Rich and Pat inside the Ueck apartment at PMSP, 1962.

Staff building with our center apartment, 1962.

Staff building recently with Ueck grandkids.

Nick the beagle, brook trout fishing on Lilly Pond, 1962.

Nick's pups, Mary Beth Audette, Rich and Pat Ueck.

Pat Ueck at Presque Isle River, 1962.

Rangers Ernest Keskinaki and George Stevens, great friends, 1963.

Knox jamison, Park Supervisor, mentor, teacher and friend. This picture is in the park's interpretive center.

CHAPTER 22
50 Years of Memory

1. Paul's Bar in Silver City where we got a Friday night burger or small steak before grocery shopping.

2. Paul Machemer's small store in Silver City where you could purchase gasoline if you couldn't get to town. Paul had bread, milk and canned goods, etc. He also sold 19¢ silver fishing spoons that I used to catch steelhead off the park shore in Lake Superior. I used a lot of them.

3. Dale's Shell Station where we fueled our Ford.

4. Gitche Gumee Oil Company where we bought our stoker coal.

5. Rudy Saari's Sporting Goods who sold us our first canoe. We called it "Red" because of it's color. He was also the Ontonagon radio disc jockey, a branch of the Ironwood radio station.

6. Hecox Hardware, the best old hardware store in the U.P.

7. The small movie theater on the main street of Ontonagon that we would take the kids to after Friday night grocery shopping. It was cold in there on winter nights.

8. Mazureks Clothing Store where I bought my first Kromer hat.

9. Labyak's, the Ford dealer, where we bought our first new Ford in 1962 and they kept it running.

10. Rosemurgy's Store where we bought our first stereo and radio combination.

I might be corrected on some of these spellings, etc., but it's been 50 years!!

Made in the USA
Charleston, SC
13 February 2014